MASTERING THE ART OF HOME FLIPPING

FOR PROFIT

A Complete quick start Guide for house flipping

MICHEAL WILSON

Copyright ©2023 by Micheal Wilson

All rights reserved, no part of this book may be produced mechanically, electronically or by any other means, including photocopying without written permission of the publisher.

Disclaimer

This book provides educational information on home flipping but is not intended as financial, legal, or professional advice. The information is based on the author's experiences and research but is subject to change. Readers should conduct their own research and seek professional advice before making investment decisions, as all investments carry risk. The author and publisher are not responsible for any losses or damages resulting from the use of this book.

Table of contents

Introduction

CHAPTER ONE
Understanding the home flipping business
Definition of Home Flipping

The History of Home Flipping

Advantages and Challenges of Flipping Homes

Types of properties that are suitable to flip

Setting Realistic Expectations and Goals

CHAPTER TWO
Finding and Evaluating Properties
Understanding Real Estate Markets

Evaluating Properties for Potential Profit

Understanding Property Conditions and Repairs

Importance of a Comprehensive Repair Plan

CHAPTER THREE
Renovating and Remodeling for Profit
Assessing the Cost of Renovations

Choosing the Right Design for Improvements

Hiring Contractors and Managing the Renovation Process

Working with Architects and Designers

Staying Within Budget and On-Schedule while renovating

CHAPTER FOUR
Financing Your Home Flip

Understanding Your Budget

Working with Lenders and Banks

Understanding the Risks of Financing

CHAPTER FIVE
Marketing and Selling Your Flip

Preparing Your Home for Sale

Utilizing Effective Marketing Strategies

Negotiating with Buyers and Closing the Sale

Dealing with Real Estate Agents and Brokers

CHAPTER SIX
Managing Risks and Challenges

Understanding Liabilities and Legal Issues

Minimizing Risks through Due Diligence

Dealing with Unexpected Problems and Setbacks

Building a Strong Support System

CHAPTER SEVEN
Building a Successful Flipping Business
Building a Network of Contacts
Scaling Your Business for Growth

Introduction

As a successful home flipper, known for my potential and ability to transform run-down properties into stunning, modern homes. It all started when I purchased my first fixer-upper property at a local auction. Despite its shabby appearance, I saw the potential for a beautiful home and threw myself into the renovation process. I worked tirelessly to gut the interior, replace the electrical and plumbing systems, and install new flooring and fixtures.

The finished product was a gorgeous, spacious home that quickly caught the eye of potential buyers. I sold the property for a significant profit and was hooked on home flipping. Over the next several years, I continued to purchase properties at auction and put my renovation skills to the test. I was able to successfully flip several more homes, each one more stunning than the last. My reputation grew, and soon I was receiving calls from real estate agents and investors seeking my expertise. Despite the challenges I faced along the way, including difficult clients and unexpected setbacks, I never lost my passion for home flipping. I saw the beauty in every property and worked tirelessly to bring it out.

One day, I received a call from a wealthy investor who was looking to purchase multiple properties for rental purposes. I saw this as an opportunity to take his home-flipping business to the next level. I formed a partnership with the investor, and together we purchased several properties in up-and-coming neighborhoods. I oversaw the renovations, and the properties were quickly rented out to eager tenants. The partnership was a huge success, and I was finally able to turn my passion for home flipping into a profitable and sustainable business. Years went by, and I became known as one of the city's most successful home flippers.

I never forgot the thrill of that first renovation project and the joy of seeing a once-dilapidated property transformed into a beautiful and modern home. I was grateful for the opportunities that had come my way and

I'm proud of the impact I had made on the real estate market. With the experience I have gathered so far in the home flipping business, I decided to put them in this book to help prospective, beginners, and expert home flippers to achieve their dreams in the home flipping business.

Are you tired of your 9-5 grind and ready to start a new and exciting venture? Have you been dreaming of becoming a successful entrepreneur and making a fortune through real estate? If so, then this book is for you!

In this comprehensive guide to home flipping for profit, you will learn how to turn your real estate dreams into a reality. I will take you through the entire process, from finding the right property to renovating it, and finally, selling it for a profit. With step-by-step guidance and practical tips, you will have everything you need to become a successful home flipper.

Think of the thrill of scouring the market for the perfect fixer-upper, envision the excitement of transforming it into a beautiful and valuable property, and imagine the satisfaction of selling it for a profit. This is what home flipping is all about, and this book will show you how to do it right.

From seasoned home flippers to complete beginners, this book has something for everyone. We will cover the latest techniques, tips, and strategies that will help you maximize your profits and minimize your risks. Whether you're looking to make a quick profit or build a long-term business, this book has all the information you need to achieve your goals.

We will start by discussing the basics of home flipping, including the different types of properties that are suitable for flipping, the costs involved, and the pros and cons of flipping. We will also cover the financing options available to you, so you can choose the best option for your situation.

Once you have a good understanding of the basics, we will delve into the technical aspects of the business. You will learn about the different renovation techniques, tools, and materials you need to complete the job, and we will provide you with step-by-step guides on how to complete various renovation tasks, such as flooring, electrical work, and painting.

Once the renovation is complete, it's time to sell the property. This is where many home flippers make the most mistakes. That's why we will provide you with the strategies you need to successfully market and sell your property, including how to price it correctly, how to stage it for maximum impact, and how to negotiate with buyers to get the best price.

We understand that the home flipping business can be challenging, but with our guidance, you will have everything you need to overcome any obstacle and achieve success. This book is not just about making money, it's about pursuing your passion and fulfilling your dreams.

So, if you're ready to start your journey to financial freedom and success in the home-flipping business, grab your copy of this book today! With its actionable advice and comprehensive coverage, you will have everything you need to become a successful home flipper and make a fortune through real estate.

CHAPTER ONE

Understanding the home flipping business

Definition of Home Flipping

Home flipping is a real estate investment strategy where an individual or group of investors purchase a property intending to renovate or improve it to sell it for a profit. The goal is to purchase a property that is undervalued, make necessary repairs and renovations, and then sell it at a higher price. The time frame for flipping a property can vary, but the average time is usually several months.

Flipping can be a lucrative business, but it also involves a significant amount of risk. The success of a home flip depends on several factors, including the location of the property, the cost of renovations, market conditions, and the demand for properties in the area. Individuals interested in home flipping need to have a solid understanding of the real estate market and construction industry, as well as a solid financial plan in place.

In addition to traditional home flipping, there are also several alternative strategies for flipping homes, such as virtual flipping, where an investor does not physically purchase or renovate a property, but instead invests in a flip through a fund or other investment vehicle.

Regardless of the strategy used, home flipping requires a significant investment of time and resources, and it's important for individuals to carefully consider their goals and risk tolerance before getting involved in the business.

The History of Home Flipping

Home flipping refers to the practice of buying a property, renovating it, and then selling it for a profit. This practice has been around for centuries but has become more popular in recent decades with the advent of home improvement shows and the growth of the real estate market. In this book, we'll take a look at the history of home flipping, from its origins to its current state.

The concept of home flipping can be traced back to the 19th century when people would buy and sell properties to make a profit. At that time, it was common for people to buy properties, fix them up, and then sell them for a profit. This was often done by people who were looking for a way to make money, or by investors who saw an opportunity to make a profit by buying and selling properties.

The practice of home flipping became more widespread in the 20th century, particularly during the post-World War II housing boom. After the war, many veterans returned home and were looking for homes to start their families. This led to a huge demand for housing, which in turn created opportunities for investors to buy, fix, and sell properties. Many of these investors became wealthy by buying and selling properties, and the practice of home flipping became more mainstream.

However, home flipping also became associated with unethical practices during this time. Some people would buy properties and then sell them quickly without making any improvements, sometimes even deliberately making them worse to sell them more cheaply. This led to a negative perception of home flipping, and many people saw it as a way to make a quick profit without any regard for the quality of the property.

The practice of home flipping took a hit in the 2008 financial crisis when the real estate market crashed and many people lost money on their investments. However, the popularity of home flipping rebounded in the years following the crisis, as the real estate market recovered and people once again saw it as a way to make a profit.

Today, home flipping is more regulated and is seen as a legitimate investment strategy. There are many resources available for people who are interested in home flipping, including online forums, books, and home improvement shows. Home flipping has become more mainstream and is seen as a way to make a profit while also improving the quality of properties.

Advantages and Challenges of Flipping Homes

Understanding both the advantages and challenges of flipping homes can help you make an informed decision about whether this type of investment is right for you. Here are some of the most notable advantages of flipping houses:

Quick Returns: One of the biggest advantages of flipping houses is the potential for quick returns. With proper planning and execution, a house flip can be completed in as little as a few months, allowing investors to quickly realize a return on their investment. This can be especially attractive for those who are looking to generate a fast return on their investment capital.

Control Over the Investment: Another advantage of flipping houses is the level of control that an investor has over the investment. Unlike other types of investments, such as stocks or bonds, the investor has direct control over the property and can make decisions regarding the renovations, marketing, and sale of the property. This level of control can allow for a greater level of customization and flexibility in the investment strategy.

Increased Value: When flipping houses, investors can take advantage of the opportunity to add value to a property through renovations and upgrades. This can include cosmetic upgrades, such as fresh paint and new flooring, as well as more significant upgrades, such as a new kitchen or bathroom. By adding value to the property, the investor can increase the asking price and ultimately realize a greater profit on the sale.

Potential Tax Benefits: Flipping houses can also offer several tax benefits. For example, expenses incurred during the renovation process, such as the cost of materials and labor, can be tax deductible. Additionally, profits realized from the sale of the property may be subject to capital gains tax, which is often lower than ordinary income tax.

Diversification: Flipping houses can also be a way to diversify an investment portfolio. By investing in real estate, investors can add a new asset class to their portfolio, which can provide a hedge against stock market volatility. This can help to reduce risk and increase the overall stability of the investment portfolio.

Hands-on Experience: Finally, flipping houses can provide hands-on experience for those who are new to real estate investing. By working on a renovation project, investors can gain valuable knowledge and skills that can be applied to future real estate investments. This can be especially valuable for novice investors who are looking to build their experience and knowledge in the real estate market.

Despite these advantages, it is important to keep in mind that flipping houses are not without its risks. For example, the cost of renovations can often be higher than expected, and there is always the possibility that the property will not sell for the expected price. Additionally, there is always the risk of market fluctuations, which can impact the value of the property.

but it's important to understand that flipping homes come with its own set of challenges, analyzed below

Finding the Right Property: One of the biggest challenges of flipping homes is finding the right property to purchase. You need to find a property that is undervalued, in a desirable location, and has the potential for renovation. The competition in the market is fierce, and you need to be quick and decisive to secure a good deal. You also need to have a good understanding of the real estate market, property values, and local zoning laws to make sure you're making a good investment.

Financing: Financing is a major challenge for many people who want to flip homes. You need to have enough money to purchase the property, pay for renovations, and cover holding costs until you can sell the property. Most banks and financial institutions are not willing to provide financing for flipping homes, so you will need to find alternative sources of funding. This may include hard money loans, private loans, or using your savings.

Budgeting: Budgeting is another challenge for those who flip homes. You need to have a clear idea of how much money you'll need for renovations and make sure you stick to your budget. If you overspend on renovations, you may not be able to make a profit when you sell the property. It's important to work with a contractor who can give you a clear estimate of the cost of renovations, and you should also factor in unexpected expenses, such as repairs to the property's foundation or fixing structural issues.

Timing: Timing is a crucial factor in flipping homes. You need to complete renovations and sell the property as quickly as possible to maximize your profits. If the renovation takes longer than expected, you will have to cover holding costs for a longer period, which can eat into your profits. You also need to time the sale of the property correctly, as the real estate market can be unpredictable. You need to sell the property when the market is strong and demand is high to maximize your profits.

Finding a Buyer: Finding a buyer is another challenge when flipping homes. You need to have a clear understanding of your target market and what they're looking for in a property. You also need to market the property effectively to attract potential buyers. This may include staging the property, taking professional photos, and listing it on real estate websites. You also need to be prepared to negotiate with potential buyers to get the best possible price for the property.

Legal Issues: Flipping homes can also come with legal issues that you need to be aware of. You need to be aware of local zoning laws, building codes, and safety regulations. You also need to make sure that all necessary permits and inspections are in order before you start renovations. Failing to follow the law can result in fines, legal action, and even the loss of your investment.

flipping homes is a challenging investment option, but it can also be very rewarding if done correctly. You need to be well-prepared, have a good understanding of the real estate market, and be willing to take calculated risks to succeed.

Types of properties that are suitable to flip

Single-family homes: Single-family homes are the most popular type of property to flip. They offer a relatively straightforward renovation process and are often in high demand, making them a good choice for flipping. Single-family homes can be purchased at a lower price, renovated to increase their value, and then sold for a profit. Some popular renovations for single-family homes include updating kitchens and bathrooms, adding new flooring, painting, and landscaping.

Multi-family homes: Multi-family homes, such as duplexes, triplexes, and fourplexes, can also be a good choice for flipping. These properties often generate higher rental income, making them a more complex but potentially more profitable investment. When flipping a multi-family home, it's important to consider the cost of renovations for each unit, as well as the potential rental income that can be generated from each unit.

Condos: Condos can also be a good choice for flipping, particularly for those looking for a lower-risk investment. Condos are often located in desirable areas, and the building's association typically takes care of exterior maintenance, freeing up the investor to focus on interior renovations. Some popular renovations for condos include updating kitchens and bathrooms, adding new flooring, and painting.

Townhouses: Townhouses are a popular choice for flipping because they offer the benefits of a single-family home combined with the convenience of a condo. Townhouses often have a lower cost of ownership than single-family homes, and the HOA typically takes care of exterior maintenance. When flipping a townhouse, it's important to consider the cost of renovations, as well as the potential resale value.

Fixer-uppers: Fixer-uppers are properties that need significant renovations. These properties can often be purchased at a discount, making them a good option for flipping. However, it's important to thoroughly analyze the cost of renovations, as well as the potential resale value, before deciding to purchase a fixer-upper. Some popular renovations for fixer-uppers include updating kitchens and bathrooms, adding new flooring, painting, and landscaping.

Distressed properties: Distressed properties, such as those in foreclosure or facing tax sales, can often be purchased at a discount. These properties can offer a good return on investment if the renovations are done properly. It's important to thoroughly research the property and the market conditions before deciding to purchase a distressed property, as the cost of renovations may be higher than expected.

Setting Realistic Expectations and Goals

flipping houses may seem like a lucrative and straightforward opportunity, but it is essential to set realistic expectations and goals to ensure success. Here are some tips for setting realistic expectations and goals in home flipping business:

Do Your Research: Before entering the home-flipping business, it is crucial to research the market and understand the current real estate trends. This includes studying the demand for different types of properties, researching the competition, and analyzing recent sales data. This will help you make informed decisions about the type of properties to invest in and the prices you can expect to sell them for.

Create a Budget: Creating a detailed budget is a critical step in home flipping. This should include all of the expenses involved in the purchase, renovation, and sale of a property. You should also factor in contingency funds to cover any unexpected expenses that may arise during the flipping process. By having a budget in place, you can ensure that you stay within your means and avoid overspending.

Set Realistic Timelines: Home flipping is not a quick process, and it is essential to set realistic timelines. This includes the time it will take to purchase a property, complete the renovations, and sell it. Make sure to take into account any unexpected delays, such as weather conditions, permit approvals, or contractor delays, which could impact your timeline.

Set Realistic Profit Margins: One of the most important aspects of home flipping is setting a realistic profit margin. This means understanding the costs involved in the flipping process, including the purchase price, renovation costs, and any other expenses, and calculating the expected profit based on the sale price. While it may be tempting to set a high-profit margin, it is essential to be realistic to ensure success.

Be Prepared for the Unexpected: No matter how much research you do or how carefully you plan, there will always be unexpected events that can impact your home-flipping business. It is essential to be prepared for these by having contingency funds set aside and being open to adjusting your expectations and goals as needed.

Work with a Team of Professionals: Home flipping can be a complex process that involves many different tasks, such as financing, legal issues, construction, and marketing. Working with a team of professionals, such as real estate agents, contractors, lawyers, and accountants, can help ensure that each aspect of the process is handled correctly and efficiently.

Keep Detailed Records: Keeping accurate and detailed records is essential to the success of a home-flipping business. This includes keeping track of expenses, such as renovation costs and marketing expenses, as well as tracking the sale price of each property. These records can help you make informed decisions about future investments and ensure that you are maximizing your profits.

Choose Properties Carefully: The success of a home-flipping business is largely dependent on choosing the right properties to invest in. When selecting a property, it is important to consider factors such as location, the potential for growth, and the overall condition of the property. It is also important to consider the cost of renovations and the potential sale price of the property.

Consider Market Trends: Understanding the current real estate market and trends is crucial when setting realistic expectations and goals for a home-flipping business. For example, if the market is slow, it may take longer to sell a property, and it may be necessary to adjust your expectations accordingly. On the other hand, if the market is strong, you may be able to sell your property quickly and at a higher price, which can help increase your profits.

Stay Adaptable: The real estate market is constantly changing, and it is essential to stay adaptable to ensure success in a home-flipping business. This means being open to adjusting your expectations and goals as needed, based on market conditions and other factors that may impact your business.

setting realistic expectations and goals is a critical aspect of success in the home flipping business. By following these tips, you can increase your chances of success and maximize your profits in this exciting and lucrative industry.

CHAPTER TWO

Finding and Evaluating Properties

Understanding Real Estate Markets

Real estate markets are dynamic and constantly evolving. Understanding these markets is crucial for success in the home-flipping business. Home flipping refers to the practice of buying a property, renovating it, and selling it for a profit within a short period, typically a few months. we'll take a look at what real estate markets are, how they affect the home flipping business, and what you need to know to succeed in this business.

What is a Real Estate Market?

A real estate market refers to the economic system in which the buying and selling of real estate take place. It is the combination of buyers, sellers, real estate agents, and various other participants that determine the price of properties in a given area. Real estate markets can be local, regional, national, or even international. Factors such as the local economy, population growth, and interest rates, among others, affect the real estate market and determine the value of properties in that market.

Supply and Demand

One of the most important concepts in real estate markets is supply and demand. When there is high demand for properties in a particular area, prices tend to rise, and when supply exceeds demand, prices tend to fall. In the home flipping business, it is important to have a good understanding of the supply and demand dynamics in the market you are operating in. If demand for properties is high, you are likely to be able to sell your renovated homes for a higher price, and if supply is high, you may have to cut your asking price to entice bidders.

Market Cycles

Real estate markets go through cycles of growth and decline. These cycles can last anywhere from a few years to a decade or more, and they are influenced by various factors such as interest rates, population growth, and the economy. In a market that is in an upward cycle, it may be easier to make a profit in the home flipping business, while in a market that is in a downward cycle, it may be more challenging. Understanding market cycles and anticipating future changes can help you make informed decisions about when and where to invest in real estate.

Location

Location is one of the most significant elements to consider when investing in real estate. Properties in desirable locations, such as those adjacent to amenities like shopping malls, public transportation, and strong schools, tend to be in higher demand and are often sold for higher prices. When flipping properties, it is crucial to carefully analyze the location of the property, since this will have a huge impact on its prospective value and resale price.

Economic Factors

The local and national economies can also have a significant impact on the real estate market. A strong economy can lead to increased demand for housing, and vice versa. Interest rates are also an important factor, as they affect the cost of borrowing and can impact the demand for housing. In a low-interest-rate environment, it is easier for buyers to obtain financing, which can lead to increased demand for housing and higher prices.

Finding Properties to Flip

Finding the right property to flip can be a challenging and time-consuming task, but it's an important step in the flipping process. To increase the chances of success and make the most profit, it's essential to do thorough research and make informed decisions.

Here are some tips on how to find properties to flip:

Determine your target market: The first step in finding properties to flip is to determine your target market. This will help you determine the type of properties you should be looking for and the area where you should be focusing your search. For example, if you're targeting first-time homebuyers, you may want to focus on properties in suburban areas with good schools and lower crime rates.

Research the area: Before you start looking for properties, research the area you're interested in. Look at real estate trends, demographic data, and economic indicators to get an idea of what the market looks like. This information can help you identify areas that are up-and-coming or in decline, which can impact the value of the properties you're interested in flipping.

Network with real estate agents: Real estate agents can be a valuable resource when it comes to finding properties to flip. They have access to properties that aren't yet on the market and can often provide you with valuable information about the area and the properties you're interested in. Build relationships with agents in your target market and let them know what you're looking for.

Look for motivated sellers: Motivated sellers are more likely to accept lower offers and are more flexible when it comes to negotiations. Some common reasons why a seller might be motivated include financial distress, divorce, death in the family, or a job transfer. You can find motivated sellers by searching online classifieds, looking for properties with signs of neglect or disrepair, or working with a real estate agent who specializes in working with motivated sellers.

Attend real estate auctions: Real estate auctions can be a great place to find properties to flip. These auctions typically include properties that are being sold as a result of foreclosure, probate, or bankruptcy. By attending auctions, you can get a sense of what properties are available and what they're selling for, which can help you make informed decisions when it comes to making an offer.

Check out online marketplaces: Online marketplaces like Zillow, Realtor.com, and Redfin can be a great place to start your search for properties to flip. These platforms allow you to search for properties based on location, price, and other criteria and can provide you with a wealth of information about the properties you're interested in, including photos, floor plans, and more.

Utilize your social network: Your social network can also be a valuable resource when it comes to finding properties to flip. Reach out to friends, family, and acquaintances and let them know what you're looking for. You never know who might know someone who is looking to sell or who has a property that would be a good fit for flipping.

Once you've found a property that you're interested in flipping, it's important to do your due diligence. This includes thoroughly inspecting the property, researching the area, and getting a clear understanding of the costs associated with the project. By taking the time to do your research and make informed decisions, you can increase your chances of success and make the most profit when flipping properties.

Evaluating Properties for Potential Profit

Evaluating properties for potential profit in home flipping is a crucial step in the process of real estate investing. To determine the profitability of a property, you need to consider several factors. Here are some steps you can follow when evaluating a property for potential profit:

Location: One of the most important factors to consider when evaluating properties for home flipping is location. Location is crucial because it determines the demand for the property, the cost of renovations, and the price you can sell it for. Look for areas with growing populations, good schools, and low crime rates. These factors will increase the value of the property and make it easier to sell. Additionally, it is important to consider the proximity of the property to public transportation, shops, and other amenities.

Property Condition: The condition of the property is another important factor to consider when evaluating properties for home flipping. Properties in good condition will require less money and time to renovate, making it easier to turn a profit. Look for properties that are structurally sound and have a good foundation. Check for any signs of water damage, mold, or other issues that could make the renovation more costly. If possible, have a professional inspect the property to determine the extent of any necessary repairs.

Renovation Costs: Renovation costs are a key factor in determining the potential profit from a home flip. The cost of the renovation should not exceed the expected return on investment. When evaluating properties, consider the cost of labor, materials, permits, and any other expenses that may be associated with the renovation. You should also consider the amount of time it will take to complete the renovation. The longer the renovation takes, the more money you will have to spend on carrying costs such as mortgage payments, utilities, and insurance.

Property Value: The value of the property is another important factor to consider when evaluating properties for home flipping. The value of the property is determined by its location, the cost of renovations, and the current market conditions. Research recent sales of similar properties in the area to determine the value of the property. This information can be found through real estate websites, local real estate agents, or a property appraisal.

Market Conditions: The current market conditions are another important factor to consider when evaluating properties for home flipping. In a hot real estate market, properties may sell quickly and for a higher price. In a slow market, it may take longer to sell the property and you may have to sell it for a lower price. Consider the current real estate market when evaluating properties.

Look for areas that are experiencing growth and are likely to appreciate over time.

Competition: Competition is another important factor to consider when evaluating properties for home flipping. Look for properties that are unique and have features that set them apart from other properties in the area. Consider properties that have large lot sizes, good views, or other special features. Properties with these features will be more attractive to potential buyers and will sell for a higher price.

Timing: Timing is also an important factor to consider when evaluating properties for home flipping. The real estate market can be unpredictable and the timing of your purchase and sale can have a significant impact on your potential profit. Try to purchase properties when the market is slow and prices are low. This will allow you to purchase the property at a lower price and sell it for a higher price when the market improves.

Financing: Financing is another important factor to consider when evaluating properties for home flipping. The cost of financing can significantly impact your potential profit. Consider the cost of a mortgage, the interest rate, and any other associated costs when evaluating properties. If you are using a mortgage to purchase the property, make sure you understand the terms and conditions of the loan, including the interest rate, loan term, and any prepayment penalties. You may also want to consider alternative financing options, such as private loans or hard money loans, which may have different terms and conditions.

Understanding Property Conditions and Repairs

One of the key aspects of successful home flipping is understanding the property's condition and the repairs that will be needed to bring it up to market standards. In this section, we will discuss the various factors involved in assessing property conditions and the importance of creating a comprehensive repair plan.

Assessing Property Condition:

The first step in home flipping is to assess the condition of the property. This involves a thorough inspection of the structure, systems, and finishes of the building. Some of the key areas to focus on include:

a. Structural Integrity: A visual inspection should be done to determine the stability and safety of the building. Look for signs of damage, such as cracks in the foundation, sagging roofs, or leaning walls.

b. Systems: The heating, cooling, electrical, and plumbing systems should be inspected to determine their current condition and whether they need repairs or upgrades.

c. Finishes: The condition of the flooring, walls, ceilings, and fixtures should be evaluated. Look for signs of wear, such as water damage, cracks, or holes.

d. Code Compliance: It is important to ensure that the property meets all local building codes and safety requirements. This may require additional repairs or upgrades.

Creating a Repair Plan:

Once the property condition has been assessed, the next step is to create a comprehensive repair plan. This plan should include:

a. Cost Estimates: The cost of each repair should be estimated, taking into account materials and labor. This will help you determine the total cost of the renovation project and determine your potential profit.

b. Prioritizing Repairs: Repairs should be prioritized based on importance, cost, and potential impact on the sale of the property. For example, structural repairs should be a higher priority than cosmetic upgrades.

c. Timing: The timeline for each repair should be established, taking into account the order in which repairs will be completed, the availability of materials and labor, and the overall timeline for the renovation project.

d. Budgeting: The repair plan should include a budget for each repair, taking into account the cost estimates and the overall budget for the renovation project.

Importance of a Comprehensive Repair Plan

A comprehensive repair plan is a crucial aspect of home flipping because it helps to ensure that the project is completed efficiently, within budget, and to the desired quality standards. A well-executed repair plan can also help to maximize the return on investment (ROI) for the flipper. Some key benefits of having a comprehensive repair plan in home flipping include:

Cost control: A comprehensive repair plan provides a clear understanding of the costs involved in the project, including materials, labor, and any necessary permits or fees. This information can help the flipper to budget appropriately and avoid costly surprises during the renovation process.

Time management: A comprehensive repair plan can help to keep the renovation project on schedule by providing a clear timeline for each stage of the project. This can help to minimize the risk of delays and ensure that the home is ready for sale within the desired timeframe.

Quality control: A comprehensive repair plan can help to ensure that the quality of the renovation work meets the desired standards. This can include specifications for materials, fixtures, and finishes, as well as guidelines for the construction process.

Improved ROI: A well-executed repair plan can help to maximize the ROI for the flipper by ensuring that the renovations are done correctly and to the desired quality standards. This can help to increase the value of the home and improve its marketability, leading to a higher sales price and a greater profit.

CHAPTER THREE

Renovating and Remodeling for Profit

Assessing the Cost of Renovations

The success of a home flipping project depends on many factors, including the cost of renovations. Understanding the cost of renovations is crucial in determining the feasibility of a home flipping project and the potential profit margin. In this chapter, we will delve into the various factors that contribute to the cost of renovations in home flipping and how to accurately estimate and budget for them.

Property Location

The location of the property is a critical factor that can significantly impact the cost of renovations. Properties in high-end neighborhoods typically have higher renovation costs due to the cost of living and the demand for premium finishes and materials. On the other hand, properties in more affordable areas may have lower renovation costs. It's essential to consider the cost of living in the area where the property is located to determine the budget for renovations.

Condition of the Property

The condition of the property can have a significant impact on the cost of renovations. Properties that are in poor condition may require extensive repairs and renovations, which can significantly increase the cost. On the other hand, properties that are in good condition may only require cosmetic upgrades, which can be done at a lower cost. Before purchasing a property, it's essential to conduct a thorough inspection to determine the extent of repairs and renovations needed.

Type of Renovations

The type of renovations you choose to undertake can also impact the cost of renovations. Basic cosmetic upgrades such as painting, new flooring, and updating fixtures and hardware can be done relatively inexpensively. More extensive renovations, such as adding rooms, expanding the kitchen or bathroom, or upgrading electrical or plumbing systems, can be more expensive. When deciding on the type of renovations to undertake, it's important to consider the cost, the potential return on investment, and the impact on the value of the property.

Materials and Labor

The cost of materials and labor is a significant factor that can impact the cost of renovations. The cost of materials and labor can vary depending on the location and the type of renovations being done. For example, using high-end materials such as granite countertops or custom cabinetry can significantly increase the cost of renovations. The same goes for labor, as hiring skilled professionals can be more expensive than using less experienced contractors.

Permits and Inspections

Depending on the scope of renovations, permits, and inspections may be required, and these can add to the cost of renovations. In most cases, permits are required for renovations that involve structural changes or electrical, plumbing, or heating and cooling upgrades. The cost of permits and inspections can vary depending on the location, so it's essential to research the specific requirements for the property you're working on.

Contingency Funds

Finally, it's essential to budget for contingency funds when estimating the cost of renovations. Contingency funds are reserves set aside for unexpected expenses that may arise during the renovation process. These can include unexpected repairs, changes in materials or labor costs, or delays in obtaining permits or inspections. A contingency fund of 10-20% of the total budget is typically recommended to ensure that you have the funds to cover unexpected expenses.

Choosing the Right Design for Improvements

The key to success in home flipping lies in choosing the right design for improvements. A well-chosen design can increase the value of the property and make it more attractive to potential buyers. On the other hand, a poorly chosen design can decrease the value of the property and make it difficult to sell.

Here are some factors to consider when choosing the right design for improvements in home flipping:

Location: The location of the property plays a major role in determining the design that will work best. The design should be in line with the style of the surrounding homes and neighborhoods. For example, a modern, contemporary design may be more appropriate for a property in a trendy, urban area, while a traditional, colonial design may be more appropriate for a property in a historic neighborhood.

Demographic: The demographic of the potential buyers should also be considered when choosing the design. Younger, single professionals may prefer a more modern, minimalist design, while families with children may prefer a more traditional, homey design.

Budget: The budget for renovations should be considered when choosing the design. Some designs may require more expensive materials or may require more extensive renovations, which could blow the budget. It's important to choose a design that fits within the budget for the renovations.

Trends: Staying up-to-date with current design trends can help make the property more attractive to potential buyers. However, it's important to keep in mind that what's popular today may not be popular in a few years, so choosing a design that is timeless and classic may be a better option.

Resale value: The design should also take into account the resale value of the property. Choosing a design that is too personal or unique may not appeal to a wide range of potential buyers, making it difficult to sell in the future.

Choosing the right design for improvements in home flipping is an important factor in determining the success of the project.

Hiring Contractors and Managing the Renovation Process

A successful renovation project depends on the quality of workmanship and the efficiency of the contractors you hire. The right team can help you turn a fixer-upper into a profitable investment, while the wrong one can result in costly mistakes, delays, and budget overruns. Here's what you need to know about hiring contractors and managing the renovation process in the home flipping business.

Determine your renovation scope and budget

Before hiring contractors, it's essential to have a clear idea of the scope of work you need to be done and how much you're willing to spend. This will help you to prioritize the tasks that need to be done, determine the type of contractors you need to hire and determine your budget. A detailed renovation plan should include a list of tasks, materials, and estimated costs.

Research and vet contractors

Once you have a clear idea of what you need, start looking for contractors. You can ask for referrals from friends, family, and business associates, search online or look for contractors who specialize in home flipping. Make sure to check references and licenses before hiring a contractor. You can also ask for a portfolio of their past work and check for reviews online.

Get bids and compare costs

Once you have a list of potential contractors, get bids from each of them. A bid should include a detailed estimate of the work, materials, and labor costs. Compare the bids and select the contractor who offers the best value for your budget. Don't forget to ask questions and clarify any unclear aspects of the bid before making a final decision.

Create a clear and detailed contract
Once you've selected a contractor, it's time to create a clear and detailed contract. The contract should include the scope of work, payment terms, deadlines, and any contingencies. Make sure to have a clear understanding of the contractor's responsibilities, warranties, and guarantees before signing the contract.

Communicate regularly with your contractor
Regular communication is essential for ensuring the success of the renovation project. Schedule regular check-ins with your contractor to review progress and address any issues that may arise. Make sure to document any changes to the scope of work and the budget in writing.

Manage your budget

Home renovation projects can be expensive, and it's essential to stick to your budget. Keep track of the costs, and make sure to review your budget regularly. If there are any changes to the scope of work, make sure to renegotiate the budget with the contractor.

Inspect the work

Regular inspections are crucial to ensure that the work is done to your standards and meets the contract specifications. Conduct regular walk-throughs with the contractor to assess the work and ensure that it meets your expectations.

Hiring contractors and managing the renovation process in the home flipping business requires careful planning and attention to detail. By following these strategies, you can ensure that your renovation project is a success and that you get a return on your investment.

Working with Architects and Designers

Partnering with Architecture and Design Professionals can play a vital role in ensuring the prosperity of a house-flipping enterprise. These professionals bring a wealth of expertise and knowledge to the table and can help turn a basic house into a show-stopper that sells for top dollar. However, it's important to understand the different roles that architects and designers play and to develop a good working relationship with them to get the most out of your investment.

Architects are responsible for the overall design and functionality of a building. They work with clients to create a design that meets their needs, while also taking into account the local building codes and zoning regulations. In the case of home flipping, an architect can help design the space to maximize its potential, making the most of the available square footage and incorporating features that are in high demand among buyers. They can also help ensure that the building meets all relevant safety and accessibility standards.

Designers, on the other hand, focus on the aesthetic aspect of the build. They work with the client to select finishes, fixtures, and materials that will help create a cohesive and attractive look throughout the home. Designers can also help choose furniture, accessories, and artwork that will complement the overall style of the home and help it stand out from the competition. In the case of home flipping, designers can play a key role in ensuring that the finished product appeals to a wide range of potential buyers, helping to increase its value.

When working with architects and designers, it's important to be clear about your goals and budget. Be sure to communicate any specific requirements you have, such as the need for additional storage or a particular floor plan. It's also important to give them plenty of time to complete their work, as rushing the design process can result in errors or oversights that can be costly to correct later on.

Another key aspect of working with architects and designers is collaboration. These professionals bring different skills and perspectives to the table, and working together can help ensure that the final product is the best it can be. It's important to be open to their suggestions and to listen to their ideas, even if they are not exactly what you had in mind. In many cases, working with an architect and designer can help you identify opportunities and solutions that you may not have considered on your own.

Finally, it's essential to establish clear lines of communication and to be responsive to their needs. This can help ensure that everyone is on the same page and that any issues that arise can be addressed promptly. Additionally, it's a good idea to establish a clear timeline and set regular check-ins to ensure that the project is progressing as planned.

Finally, working with architects and designers can be a valuable investment in a home-flipping business. By leveraging their expertise, you can create a home that is both functional and aesthetically appealing, helping to increase its value and make it more appealing to potential buyers. Just be sure to communicate clearly, collaborate effectively, and establish a good working relationship to get the most out of your investment.

Staying Within Budget and On-Schedule while renovating

Renovating a property for flipping purposes can be an exciting but challenging task, as it requires careful planning and budget management to ensure the project stays on schedule and within budget. In this article, we will discuss some tips to help you stay within budget and on schedule while renovating your home flipping project.

Set a realistic budget: Before starting the renovation project, it is important to determine the amount of money you have to spend. This includes not only the cost of materials, but also labor, permits, and any other miscellaneous expenses that may arise during the renovation process. To avoid overspending, set a budget that is realistic and takes into account all of the expenses you will incur.

Make a list of priorities: Once you have a budget in place, make a list of the most important renovation tasks that need to be completed. This will help you focus on the most critical tasks and avoid unnecessary spending.

Shop around for the best deals: To stay within budget, it is important to shop around for the best deals on materials, tools, and labor. Take the time to research and compare prices from different suppliers to ensure you are getting the best deal possible.

Hire professionals: While it may be tempting to try to save money by doing the work yourself, it is important to consider the cost of time and potential mistakes. Hiring professionals can help ensure the work is done efficiently and to a high standard, which can ultimately save you time and money in the long run.

Plan for unexpected expenses: No matter how well you plan, there will always be unexpected expenses that arise during the renovation process. To prepare for these, set aside a contingency fund in your budget to cover any unanticipated expenses.

Set a timeline: To stay on schedule, it is important to establish a timeline for the renovation process. This will help you keep track of progress and ensure the project stays on schedule. Be sure to factor in time for unexpected setbacks and delays, as these are bound to happen during any renovation project.

Regularly monitor progress: Regularly monitoring progress is an important part of staying on schedule and within budget. Regular check-ins with contractors, suppliers, and other involved parties will help keep everyone on track and ensure that the project stays on schedule.

Stay flexible: While it is important to have a plan in place, it is equally important to remain flexible. If something unexpected comes up, be prepared to adjust your plan accordingly. The most important thing is to stay within budget and on schedule, so be willing to make changes as needed.

CHAPTER FOUR

Financing Your Home Flip

Understanding Your Budget

Residential flipping has gained notoriety in the property sector as a profitable venture where investors purchase a house, implement necessary renovations and modifications, and then resell it for a gain. It necessitates substantial financial resources and one of the fundamental aspects of success in home flipping is having a comprehensive comprehension of your financial plan. A thoroughly planned budget will assist you in maintaining your progress and making knowledgeable choices throughout the flipping journey. We will delve into the crucial elements of comprehending your budget in the realm of home flipping.

Start with the Purchase Price

The first step in creating a budget for your home flipping project is to determine the purchase price of the property. This will be the foundation of your budget, and it will inform your other financial decisions. When looking at potential properties to flip, consider their location, the current real estate market conditions, and the overall condition of the property. This information will help you determine the purchase price and make an informed decision on whether the property is a good investment opportunity.

Estimate the Cost of Repairs and Upgrades

Once you have the purchase price, you need to estimate the cost of repairs and upgrades. This will include things like roof repair, kitchen or bathroom remodels, new flooring, painting, and any necessary structural repairs. Be sure to factor in the cost of materials and labor, as well as any permits or inspections that may be required. It is also important to have a contingency plan for unexpected expenses that may arise during the flipping process.

Consider Holding Costs

Holding costs are expenses that occur while you own the property, but before it is sold. These costs may include mortgage payments, property taxes, insurance, and utilities. It's important to factor these costs into your budget as they can add up quickly and eat into your profit margin.

Determine the Sales Price

Once you have a good understanding of the costs associated with the flipping project, you can determine the sales price. The sales price should be based on the estimated market value of the property after repairs and upgrades have been completed. It's important to be realistic about the sales price, as overpricing can result in the property taking longer to sell, and underpricing can leave money on the table.

Plan for Marketing and Closing Costs

In addition to the costs associated with purchasing and upgrading the property, there are also costs associated with selling it. These include marketing costs, such as photography and advertising, and closing costs, such as real estate agent commissions and title fees. It's important to factor these costs into your budget, as they can impact your overall profit margin.

Regularly Review and Adjust Your Budget
As you move through the home flipping process, it's important to regularly review and adjust your budget as necessary. This will help ensure that you stay on track and make informed decisions. Additionally, it's important to be flexible and willing to make changes to your budget if circumstances change.

Types of Financing for Home Flips

securing the necessary funding for a home flip can be challenging, especially for first-time investors who may not have a lot of money saved up. Fortunately, there are several types of financing options available for home flippers, each with its benefits and drawbacks.

Cash Financing: This is the most straightforward type of financing, where the home flipper uses their savings or other liquid assets to fund the purchase and renovation of the property. The advantage of cash financing is that there is no interest to pay, no approval process to go through, and the home flipper has complete control over the project. However, using cash financing limits the size and number of projects that a home flipper can take on since they have to be able to pay for the entire investment upfront.

Hard Money Loans: Hard money loans are a type of financing that is offered by private lenders who specialize in funding real estate projects. Unlike traditional loans, hard money loans are based on the value of the property being invested in, rather than the borrower's creditworthiness. These loans come with higher interest rates and fees, but they offer a faster approval process, making them an ideal choice for real estate investors who need to act quickly. With hard money loans, investment projects can be approved in just a few days, making them a popular choice for home flippers.

Line of Credit: A line of credit is a loan that allows the borrower to access funds as needed, up to a certain limit. Home flippers can use a line of credit to cover the costs of a home flip, such as the purchase price, renovation costs, and other expenses. The advantage of a line of credit is that the home flipper only pays interest on the amount they borrow, and can access the funds as needed throughout the project. However, the approval process for a line of credit can take several weeks, so it's not ideal for home flippers who need to move quickly on a project.

Traditional Bank Loan: A traditional bank loan is a loan provided by a commercial bank or other financial institution. Home flippers can use a traditional bank loan to finance a home flip, but the approval process can be lengthy, and the loan may require a higher credit score, a larger down payment, or other stringent requirements. The advantage of a traditional bank loan is that it typically has a lower interest rate compared to hard money loans, making it a more cost-effective option for home flippers who have the time to wait for the approval.

Joint Venture Financing: Joint venture financing is a partnership between two or more individuals who pool their resources to finance a home flip. In a joint venture, one partner provides the funding, while the other partner manages the project. Joint venture financing can be a win-win for both partners, as the partner who provides the funding can earn a profit without having to manage the project, while the partner who manages the project can earn a share of the profits without having to provide all of the funding.

There are several types of financing options available for home flippers, each with its advantages and disadvantages. Home flippers should carefully consider their individual needs, goals, and financial situation before choosing the right type of financing for their home flip.

Working with Lenders and Banks

Collaborating with financial institutions and banking organizations can be a vital aspect of the house flipping industry, as they can furnish the required funding for buying and modernizing properties. The following are some essential points to keep in mind while working with lenders and banks in the home flipping business:

Understanding the different types of loans: There are several types of loans available for the home-flipping business, including conventional loans, hard money loans, and bridge loans. Conventional loans are provided by banks and are typically the most affordable, but have strict requirements, such as a minimum credit score and a large down payment. Hard money loans are provided by private investors and are typically more expensive, but can be easier to qualify for and offer more flexible terms. Bridge loans are short-term loans used to finance the purchase and renovation of a property until it can be sold for a profit.

Building a good credit history: To qualify for a loan from a bank, it is important to have a good credit history and a solid financial track record. This may include paying bills on time, having a steady income, and avoiding excessive debt.

Developing a business plan: Before approaching a lender or a bank, it is important to have a clear and well-defined business plan. This plan should outline the objectives of your home flipping business, the properties you plan to acquire, the budget for renovations, the estimated timeline for completion, and the expected return on investment. Having a solid business plan can demonstrate your commitment and increase your chances of getting a loan.

Establishing a relationship with a lender or a bank: Building a relationship with a lender or a bank can help you secure financing for your home-flipping business.

This can include meeting with loan officers, providing updates on your business, and demonstrating your success. Lenders and banks are more likely to work with individuals or businesses that have established a track record of success and have shown that they are trustworthy and responsible.

Staying organized and keeping records: Keeping accurate and detailed records of your expenses and income can help you manage your finances and increase your credibility with lenders and banks. This can include maintaining a budget, tracking expenses, and keeping receipts and invoices.

Understanding the Risks of Financing

Home flipping, the act of buying, renovating, and reselling a property within a short period, has become a popular investment strategy in recent years. While it can be a lucrative business, it also comes with significant risks that investors need to understand. Let's explore the risks involved in financing a home-flipping business and what investors can do to mitigate those risks.

Market Risks: The real estate market is highly cyclical and subject to fluctuations in supply and demand. Home flippers need to have a good understanding of the market trends and conditions in the area where they plan to invest. If the market turns against them, they may not be able to sell the property for a profit or sell it at all, leaving them with a property that is difficult to finance and maintain.

Financing Risks: Financing is a crucial part of the home flipping business, as investors typically need to borrow money to purchase the property and pay for the renovation costs. However, there are several risks associated with financing, including interest rate fluctuations, changes in lending policies, and credit market disruptions. Additionally, lenders may require that the property be refinanced after the renovation work is completed, which can lead to higher costs and decreased profits.

Renovation Risks: Home flipping often involves significant renovation work, and this work is not always cheap. In addition to the costs associated with the renovation itself, investors need to consider the risks of unexpected delays, cost overruns, and the quality of the work being performed. If the renovation work is not completed on time or is of poor quality, it can negatively impact the value of the property and make it difficult to sell.

Legal Risks: Home flipping also involves several legal risks, including zoning and building code violations, disputes with contractors, and title issues. Investors need to be aware of these risks and take steps to minimize their exposure, such as conducting thorough due diligence on the property and the contractors involved in the renovation.

Timing Risks: Timing is critical in the home flipping business, as investors need to make quick decisions and act quickly to purchase and renovate the property. If they take too long, they may miss out on a good opportunity or run into problems with financing or renovation. On the other hand, if they move too quickly, they may end up overpaying for the property or making mistakes during the renovation process that can negatively impact the value of the property.

Reputation Risks: Home flipping can also involve reputation risks, as investors need to maintain a good reputation in the community to attract buyers and buyers' agents. If the home flipper is seen as unethical or unreliable, it can impact their ability to sell the property and negatively impact their reputation in the community.

Environmental Risks: Properties that have been abandoned for a long period or properties that have been used for commercial purposes may have environmental issues, such as lead paint, asbestos, or mold. These environmental hazards can significantly impact the cost of renovation and make the property difficult to sell. Investors need to be aware of these risks and take steps to mitigate them, such as conducting environmental assessments and obtaining professional advice from environmental experts.

To mitigate these risks, home flippers need to do their homework and carefully consider all of the factors involved in their investment. This includes researching the real estate market, obtaining professional advice from a real estate agent or a financial advisor, and carefully reviewing all loan documents and contracts. Additionally, investors should have a contingency plan in place in case the investment does not go as planned, such as having a backup source of financing or a contingency plan for selling the property if necessary.

CHAPTER FIVE

Marketing and Selling Your Flip

Preparing Your Home for Sale

Getting your home ready for listing is an integral part of the home flipping industry. The objective is to present the property desirably to prospective buyers with the hope of realizing a profit. To achieve this, there are several preparations you can make to enhance the appeal of your home and attract potential buyers, including:

Clean and declutter: Start by thoroughly cleaning the home, both inside and out. This includes washing windows, cleaning carpets and flooring, and wiping down surfaces. Decluttering is also important because potential buyers want to see the space and imagine themselves living in the home. Remove excess furniture and personal items, and consider renting a storage unit to store items you don't need.

Make repairs: Identify any repairs that need to be made, both big and small. This includes fixing leaky faucets, repairing damaged walls, and replacing worn-out flooring. These repairs will not only make the home more appealing, but they can also help increase the home's value.

Paint and update: Breathe new life into your home with a fresh coat of paint. Opt for neutral shades that will attract a broad range of prospective buyers. Upgrade outdated features, such as lighting fixtures and cabinet hardware, to give your home a contemporary appearance. These simple updates can have a big impact on the overall look and feel of your home.

Stage the home: Staging involves arranging furniture and decor to make the home look as appealing and spacious as possible. This can include rearranging furniture, removing clutter, and adding decor elements like flowers and rugs. Hiring a professional stager can be a worthwhile investment, as they have experience in making homes look their best.

Improve curb appeal: The exterior of the home is just as important as the interior. Make sure the lawn is trimmed, the garden is well-maintained, and the exterior of the home is cleaned and painted if necessary. These small changes can make a big difference in attracting potential buyers.

Price it right: Pricing your home correctly is essential to selling it quickly and for the best possible price. Do your research to determine the market value of similar homes in the area, and price your home competitively.

Enhance your prospects of a successful sale by following these tips to make your home more attractive to prospective buyers. The objective is to establish a warm and welcoming atmosphere that enables potential buyers to envision themselves residing in the space.

Utilizing Effective Marketing Strategies

Marketing is a crucial aspect of any business, including the home flipping industry. By utilizing effective marketing strategies, you can reach potential buyers, showcase the unique features and benefits of your property, and ultimately sell it for a profit. From online advertising to traditional real estate marketing methods, there are numerous options available to help you effectively market your property. Let's explore some of the most effective marketing strategies you can use to help you reach your goals.

Utilize Real Estate Listing Websites: One of the most effective ways to reach potential buyers is by utilizing real estate listing websites. These websites allow you to list your property and reach a large audience of interested buyers. Some popular websites include Zillow, Redfin, and Realtor.com. Make sure to provide high-quality photos and descriptions of your property to attract potential buyers.

Leverage Social Media: Social media platforms, such as Facebook, Instagram, and Twitter, can be powerful tools for marketing your properties. Create a social media page for your business and post updates about your latest flip projects, before-and-after photos, and other relevant content. This will not only help you reach a larger audience but also allow you to engage with potential buyers and build your brand.

Use Direct Mail Marketing: Direct mail marketing involves sending marketing materials, such as flyers or postcards, directly to potential buyers. This can be a cost-effective way to reach potential buyers who live in the area where your property is located. Make sure to target your direct mail marketing efforts to individuals who are likely to be interested in buying a home, such as first-time homebuyers or those who have recently sold their property.

Host Open Houses: Hosting open houses is a great way to showcase your property and give potential buyers a chance to see the renovations you have made. Make sure to promote your open house through social media, direct mail marketing, and other marketing channels to reach as many potential buyers as possible.

Partner with Local Realtors: Realtors can be valuable partners in your home-flipping business as they have access to a large network of potential buyers. Consider partnering with local realtors who specialize in selling homes in your target market. You can offer them a commission on any sale they help close, and they can provide valuable marketing and sales support to help you sell your properties.

successful marketing tactics are pivotal for achievement in the residential flipping industry. Employing property listing websites, capitalizing on social media platforms, utilizing direct mail advertising, conducting open house events, and collaborating with nearby real estate agents are all effective methods that can assist you in connecting with prospective buyers and optimizing your profits. By executing these tactics and continually refining your marketing technique, you can establish a thriving home flipping business that produces steady earnings."

Negotiating with Buyers and Closing the Sale

Negotiating with buyers and successfully closing the sale are important steps in the home flipping process. As the seller, it is important to understand the buyer's perspective and make informed decisions that will help you reach a mutually beneficial agreement. Here's a guide on how to effectively negotiate and close the sale with buyers.

Research the Market: Before negotiating with a buyer, it's important to know the market conditions and the average price for similar properties in the area. This information will give you an idea of what to expect in terms of offers and help you make informed decisions during negotiations.

Know your Numbers: It's essential to have a clear understanding of the costs involved in the flipping process, including the purchase price, renovation costs, and holding costs. This information will help you determine the minimum price you can accept for the property.

Set your Asking Price: Based on your research, set an asking price that is competitive but still allows for a profit. It's important to keep in mind that the asking price doesn't have to be the final sale price, as this is where negotiations come into play.

Be Prepared to Negotiate: When negotiating with buyers, it's important to listen to their concerns and be willing to make compromises. For example, if a buyer is hesitant about the asking price, you may offer to cover some closing costs or provide a home warranty.

Use Emotional Appeal: Buyers are often more willing to pay a higher price if they have a personal connection to the property. Highlight the unique features and selling points of the property to make an emotional appeal to the buyer.

Close the Deal: Once you have reached a mutually agreeable price and terms, it's time to close the deal. This typically involves signing a purchase and sale agreement and transferring ownership of the property to the buyer.

Follow-Up: After closing the sale, it's important to follow up with the buyer to ensure that everything is going smoothly. This is also a good opportunity to ask for a referral or positive review, which can help you build your reputation as a successful home flipper.

In conclusion, negotiating with buyers and closing the sale is a key step in the home flipping business. By being prepared, being flexible, and using emotional appeal, you can successfully close the sale and make a profit on your flip.

Dealing with Real Estate Agents and Brokers

Dealing with real estate agents and brokers can be an important aspect of the home-flipping business. Real estate professionals can provide valuable expertise, connections, and resources that can help you find the right property, negotiate a good deal, and manage the sales process efficiently. However, it is important to understand the different roles that agents and brokers play and how to work with them effectively to ensure a successful home-flipping project.

Real Estate Agents:

Real estate agents have licensed professionals who work for real estate brokerages and help clients buy, sell, and rent properties. They typically earn a commission based on the sale price of a property. When working with real estate agents in a home-flipping business, it is important to be upfront about your goals and expectations. For example, if you are looking for a property to flip, you may want to tell the agent that you are looking for a fixer-upper property at a good price. This will help the agent understand what you are looking for and provide you with relevant listings.

Brokers:

Brokers are licensed professionals who oversee the work of real estate agents and are responsible for the licensing and compliance of their brokerage. They typically have more experience and expertise than agents and can provide valuable advice and support throughout the home flipping process. When working with brokers, it is important to build a relationship based on trust and mutual respect. This can be accomplished by being transparent about your goals and expectations, and by working together to achieve a successful outcome.

Negotiating Commission:

When it comes to working with real estate agents and brokers, negotiating the commission for their services is a common practice. The commission usually consists of a percentage of the property's sale price and is paid by the seller. In the context of a home-flipping business, it's crucial to establish a fair and reasonable commission that reflects the worth of the real estate professional's contributions. This can encompass their knowledge, network, and assets.

Finding the Right Agent or Broker:

To find the right real estate agent or broker for your home-flipping business, it is important to do your research and speak with multiple professionals. You can start by asking for referrals from friends, family, or other real estate professionals. You can also search online and read reviews of different agents and brokers to get a sense of their experience, reputation, and success rate. Once you have found a few potential candidates, it is important to meet with them in person to discuss your goals and expectations and to see if they are a good fit for your needs.

Dealing with real estate agents and brokers can be a valuable aspect of the home-flipping business. These professionals can provide valuable expertise, connections, and resources that can help you find the right property, negotiate a good deal, and manage the sales process efficiently. However, it is important to understand the different roles that agents and brokers play and how to work with them effectively to ensure a successful home-flipping project. By doing your research, negotiating a fair commission, and finding the right professional for your needs, you can maximize the benefits of working with real estate agents and brokers in your home-flipping business.

CHAPTER SIX

Managing Risks and Challenges

Understanding Liabilities and Legal Issues

In the home flipping business, it's important to be aware of potential liabilities and legal issues that may arise. From understanding building codes and regulations to managing contracts and liability insurance, there are numerous considerations to keep in mind when flipping homes. By being informed about the legal aspects of the business, you can mitigate potential risks and avoid costly mistakes. Failure to properly manage these risks can result in significant financial losses, legal problems, and reputational damage.

Liability Issues:

Health and Safety Concerns: Home flippers have a legal obligation to ensure that the properties they purchase are safe and habitable. This means that they must address any health and safety hazards, such as mold, asbestos, lead paint, or structural problems. If the property is found to be unsafe and the flipper has not addressed the issue, they can be held liable for any injury or harm that results.

Zoning and Permit Requirements: Home flippers must comply with all local zoning and building codes, including obtaining the necessary permits for renovations. Failing to comply with these regulations can result in fines, legal action, and the possibility of having to undo the renovations.

Environmental Concerns: Home flippers must also be aware of any environmental issues that may affect the property, such as contaminated soil or groundwater. If these issues are not addressed, the flipper can be held responsible for any environmental damage that results.

Legal Issues:

Contracts and Closing Documents: When purchasing a property, it is important to carefully review all contracts and closing documents to ensure that there are no hidden liens or other legal issues that could affect the sale.

Title Issues: Home flippers must ensure that the property has a clear title, meaning that there are no liens or other claims on the property. If there are title issues, the flipper may not be able to sell the property or may have to pay off the liens before the sale can be completed.

Fraud and Misrepresentation: Home flippers must ensure that they are not the victims of fraud or misrepresentation when purchasing a property. For example, if the seller misrepresents the condition of the property, the flipper may be able to seek compensation for any damages that result.

Additionally, it's also important to consider insurance options when flipping homes. Home flippers should consider getting liability insurance to protect against lawsuits, property damage, and personal injury claims. Insurance can provide financial protection against unexpected costs and help ensure that the flipping project remains profitable.

It is also important to keep accurate and detailed records throughout the home flipping process. This includes documentation of all expenses related to the purchase, renovation, and sale of the property. This information can help in the event of a dispute or audit and can also be used to determine the profitability of the project.

It is also important to be aware of any tax implications that may arise from home flipping. Home flippers may be required to pay capital gains taxes on their profits, and it's important to understand the tax laws in the jurisdiction in which the property is located.

Minimizing Risks through Due Diligence

Home flipping comes with various risks and uncertainties. Minimizing these risks is crucial for success in this industry, and this is where due diligence comes in. However, it is not without risks, and due diligence is an important step in minimizing those risks and ensuring a successful investment.

Due diligence is the process of thoroughly researching and evaluating a potential investment to identify any potential problems or risks. This can include reviewing property records, inspections, and market analysis.

In the context of home flipping, due diligence should start with a thorough evaluation of the property itself. This includes a comprehensive home inspection, which can identify any hidden issues such as structural problems, electrical or plumbing issues, and pest infestations. In addition, the local zoning laws and building codes should be reviewed to ensure that any planned renovations are in compliance and won't result in costly fines or legal issues.

Market analysis is also crucial in home flipping. This includes researching the local real estate market to determine the current trends and potential resale values. This will help investors determine the budget and timeline for the renovation and help them determine the best strategy for selling the property. Additionally, understanding the local housing market can help investors determine if it is a good time to buy and sell and if there is a strong demand for the type of property they are considering.

Another important aspect of due diligence is reviewing the financial records of the property. This includes checking the property's tax records and assessing the current mortgage, if there is one, to determine the potential financial liabilities. In addition, investors should also consider ongoing expenses, such as property insurance, property taxes, and utilities, to ensure that these costs do not negatively impact the profitability of the investment.

Finally, it is important to consider the legal and regulatory issues involved in home flipping. This includes understanding the contract terms and the obligations of both the buyer and the seller, as well as any potential legal liabilities or disputes that may arise.

Dealing with Unexpected Problems and Setbacks

Home flipping can be a highly profitable endeavor, but it is not without its risks and obstacles. The process involves purchasing a property, renovating it, and then selling it for a profit. However, various challenges can arise during the renovation process, such as unforeseen budget overruns, permitting difficulties, and structural issues. It is imperative for anyone considering home flipping to be prepared for these challenges and to have a plan for mitigating them to increase their chances of success.

One of the most common issues that home flippers face is a budget overrun. Renovations often cost more than initially planned, and this can lead to financial difficulties. To prevent this from happening, it is important to create a detailed budget that takes into account all of the costs associated with the project, including materials, labor, permits, and any unexpected expenses that may arise. Additionally, it is helpful to have a contingency plan in place, such as a line of credit or an investment partner, to cover any additional costs that may arise during the renovation process.

Permitting issues can also be a major setback in the home flipping process. Zoning laws and building codes can be complex, and it is important to ensure that all necessary permits and approvals are obtained before beginning any work on the property. To avoid permitting issues, it is advisable to consult with a professional, such as a real estate attorney or a contractor, who can help navigate the permitting process and ensure that all regulations are followed.

Unexpected structural problems are another challenge that home flippers may face. For example, the property may have hidden damage such as termite infestations, mold, or foundation issues that are not apparent until the renovation process begins. To mitigate the risk of encountering these types of issues, it is important to thoroughly inspect the property before making a purchase and to be prepared to budget for any necessary repairs that may be required.

Another common setback in home flipping is the delay in the renovation or construction process. This can be due to a variety of reasons, such as inclement weather, supply chain disruptions, or issues with contractors or subcontractors. To prevent delays from affecting the project timeline, it is important to have a well-planned schedule that takes into account any potential roadblocks and to have backup plans in place to keep the project moving forward even if there are unexpected setbacks.

It is also important to stay organized and keep accurate records throughout the home-flipping process. This includes keeping track of all expenses, such as material and labor costs, as well as any changes to the project timeline or budget. This information will be helpful in the event of any disputes or disagreements with contractors or subcontractors, and it will also provide a clear picture of the project's progress and financial status.

Good communication is also key to overcoming unexpected problems and setbacks in home flipping. This includes regular communication with contractors, subcontractors, and other stakeholders involved in the project, as well as keeping the property's future buyers informed about any changes or delays that may impact the completion of the project. Regular communication helps to build trust and keep everyone on the same page, which can help to minimize the impact of unexpected problems and setbacks.

Finally, it is important to remain flexible and open to alternative solutions. Sometimes, unexpected problems or setbacks may require a different approach, and being open to alternative solutions can help to minimize the impact of these challenges and keep the project moving forward. For example, if there is a delay in obtaining the necessary permits, it may be possible to temporarily pivot to another aspect of the renovation process, such as landscaping or interior design, to keep the project on track.

In conclusion, home flipping is a complex process that requires careful planning, attention to detail, and the ability to adapt to unexpected problems and setbacks. By being prepared, staying organized, maintaining good communication, and being flexible, home flippers can overcome these challenges and achieve success in their home-flipping ventures.

Building a Strong Support System

The potential for the financial gain of this investment is high, the process of home flipping can be challenging and stressful. Building a strong support system is essential for success in the home-flipping business.

A support system can consist of various individuals and resources, including family, friends, business partners, contractors, real estate agents, and financial advisors. Here are some tips for building a strong support system in home flipping:

Partner with experienced professionals: Partnering with experienced professionals, such as real estate agents, contractors, and financial advisors, can provide valuable insight and expertise to help guide you through the home flipping process. These individuals can also help you make informed decisions, stay on track, and avoid costly mistakes.

Build a network of trusted contacts: Building a network of trusted contacts, including friends, family, and business partners, can provide a valuable source of support and resources. This network can provide help with tasks such as financing, marketing, and renovation, and can also provide a sounding board for ideas and feedback.

Utilize technology and tools: Technology and tools, such as project management software, can help streamline the home flipping process and make it easier to keep track of progress and budgets. These tools can also help you stay organized and keep all parties involved in the loop.

Maintain open communication: Communication is key when it comes to building a strong support system in home flipping. Regularly checking in with partners, contractors, and others involved in the project can help ensure that everyone is on the same page and can help resolve any issues that may arise.

Seek out support groups: Joining a support group, such as a local real estate investment club, can provide a valuable source of support and resources. These groups often include experienced home flippers who can offer advice and guidance, as well as networking opportunities with other professionals in the industry.

Establish clear roles and responsibilities: When working with partners or a team, it is important to establish clear roles and responsibilities to ensure that everyone is on the same page. This can help avoid misunderstandings and ensure that the project is completed smoothly and efficiently.

Develop a contingency plan: Home flipping projects can be unpredictable, and it is important to have a contingency plan in place in case something goes wrong. This can include having backup contractors, alternate financing options, and a plan for handling unexpected expenses.

Foster positive relationships: Building positive relationships with everyone involved in the home flipping project, including contractors, real estate agents, and partners, can help ensure a successful outcome. Treating everyone with respect, fairness, and professionalism can help foster positive relationships that can last beyond the current project.

Seek feedback and advice: Regularly seeking feedback and advice from your support system can help you stay on track and make informed decisions. This can help you identify areas for improvement and make changes to your approach, ensuring that you stay competitive and successful in the home-flipping business.

Continuously educate yourself: Finally, it is important to continuously educate yourself about the home flipping industry. Staying up-to-date with the latest trends, technologies, and market conditions can help you make informed decisions and stay ahead of the competition.

CHAPTER SEVEN

Building a Successful Flipping Business

Building a Network of Contacts

Building a network of contacts is essential in the home-flipping business. This network will be the foundation of your business and will help you succeed in this competitive industry. In this part of this book, I will discuss several strategies to help you build a strong network of contacts in the home-flipping business.

Attend Networking Events: Attending networking events such as real estate conferences, trade shows, and local meetups is a great way to meet potential partners, suppliers, and contractors. These events offer an opportunity to connect with industry professionals and make lasting connections. You can also join local real estate clubs or organizations to further expand your network.

Leverage Social Media: Social media platforms such as LinkedIn, Facebook, and Twitter are powerful tools for building a network of contacts. They allow you to connect with people in your industry and share your expertise. You can also join groups and participate in discussions related to real estate and home flipping. This will help you build a strong online presence and increase your exposure to potential contacts.

Partner with Other Investors: Partnering with other investors can be a great way to build a network of contacts. By working together, you can share resources and knowledge, as well as pool your resources to take on bigger projects. You can also refer businesses to each other, which can help you build a strong reputation in the industry.

Connect with Real Estate Agents: Real estate agents are a valuable source of information and can help you find great deals on properties. Building a strong relationship with real estate agents can help you access a larger pool of properties and increase your chances of finding the perfect property to flip.

Collaborate with Contractors: Contractors are an essential part of the home flipping business, and having a strong network of reliable contractors can make or break your success. Building a relationship with contractors can help you get better pricing and better workmanship, as well as give you access to new projects.

Utilize Online Communities: Online communities such as forums and discussion boards can be a great way to connect with other investors, contractors, and real estate agents. By participating in these communities, you can build relationships and gain valuable insights into the industry.

building a network of contacts in the home flipping business takes time and effort. But by utilizing these strategies, you can create a strong foundation for your business that will help you succeed in this competitive industry. Remember to always be professional, helpful, and open to new connections, and your network will grow organically over time.

Scaling Your Business for Growth

Scaling a home-flipping business can be a challenging but rewarding process. The goal of scaling is to increase the size and reach of the business while maintaining profitability and efficiency. Here are some steps to help you scale your home flipping business for growth:

Develop a comprehensive business plan: A well-constructed business blueprint can assist you in charting out your objectives, recognizing the assets required, and deciding on the most effective methods to attain success. It should also encompass a marketing approach, financial strategy, and a plan to handle potential risks.

Increase your network: Networking is essential for finding new deals, building relationships with contractors, and connecting with potential investors. Attend industry events, join local real estate clubs, and build relationships with real estate agents and brokers.

Hire a team: As your business grows, you will need to hire a team to help with the day-to-day operations. Consider hiring a project manager, a real estate agent, a bookkeeper, and a contractor.

Streamline processes: As your business grows, it's important to streamline processes to increase efficiency and reduce costs. Consider investing in project management software, a CRM system, and construction management software to help you stay organized and on top of your projects.

Enhance your marketing efforts: A strong marketing plan is crucial for attracting new business and building brand awareness. Consider investing in online and offline marketing efforts, such as social media advertising, email marketing, and direct mail campaigns.

Expand your financing options: As your business grows, it's important to have access to the capital you need to fund your projects. Consider working with private lenders, hard money lenders, and crowdfunding platforms to help you secure the financing you need.

Diversify your portfolio: Diversifying your portfolio can help reduce your risk and increase your profitability. Consider expanding into other real estate markets, investing in rental properties, or developing a new product line.

Continuously evaluate and refine your strategies: Continuously evaluating and refining your strategies is key to success in any business. Regularly review your performance, gather feedback from your team and customers, and make adjustments as needed to ensure you are on track to meet your goals.

Scaling a home-flipping business can be a complex process, but with the right strategies in place, you can increase your reach, grow your business, and achieve long-term success.

Made in United States
Orlando, FL
03 September 2024

51098976R10065